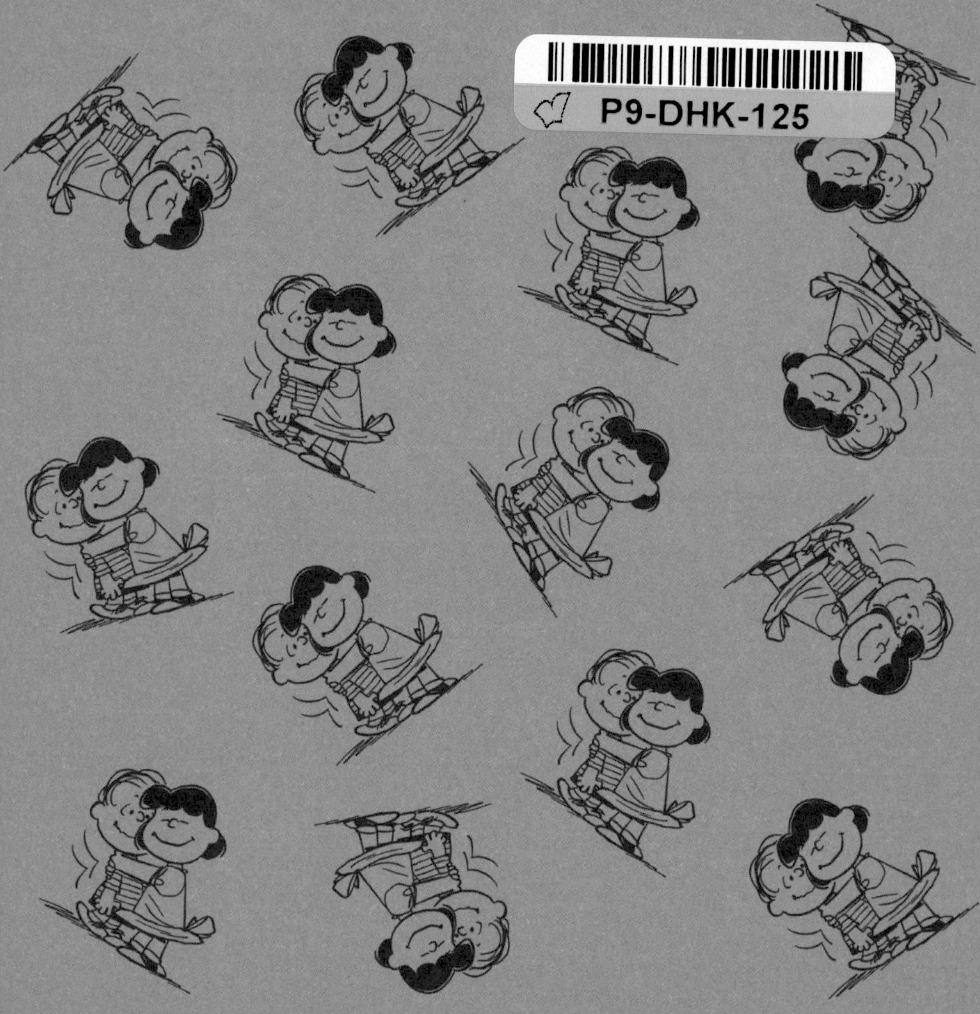

CHRISTMAS
IS
TOGETHER-TIME
BY
CHARLES M.
SCHULZ

ISBN-13: 978-1-933662-37-4
ISBN-10: 1-933662-37-9

This book may be ordered by mail from the publisher.
Please include $4.50 for postage and handling.
But please support your local bookseller first!

Books published by Cider Mill Press Book Publishers are available at special discounts
for bulk purchases in the United States by corporations, institutions, and other
organizations. For more information, please contact the publisher.

Cider Mill Press Book Publishers
"Where good books are ready for press"
12 Port Farm Road
Kennebunkport, Maine 04046

Visit us on the web!
www.cidermillpress.com

Design by: Jason Zamajtuk

Printed in China

1 2 3 4 5 6 7 8 9 10

A PEANUTS CLASSIC Edition

CHRISTMAS
IS
TOGETHER-TIME

Christmas is the decorations that go up on the day after Halloween . . . and Thanksgiving isn't even here yet!

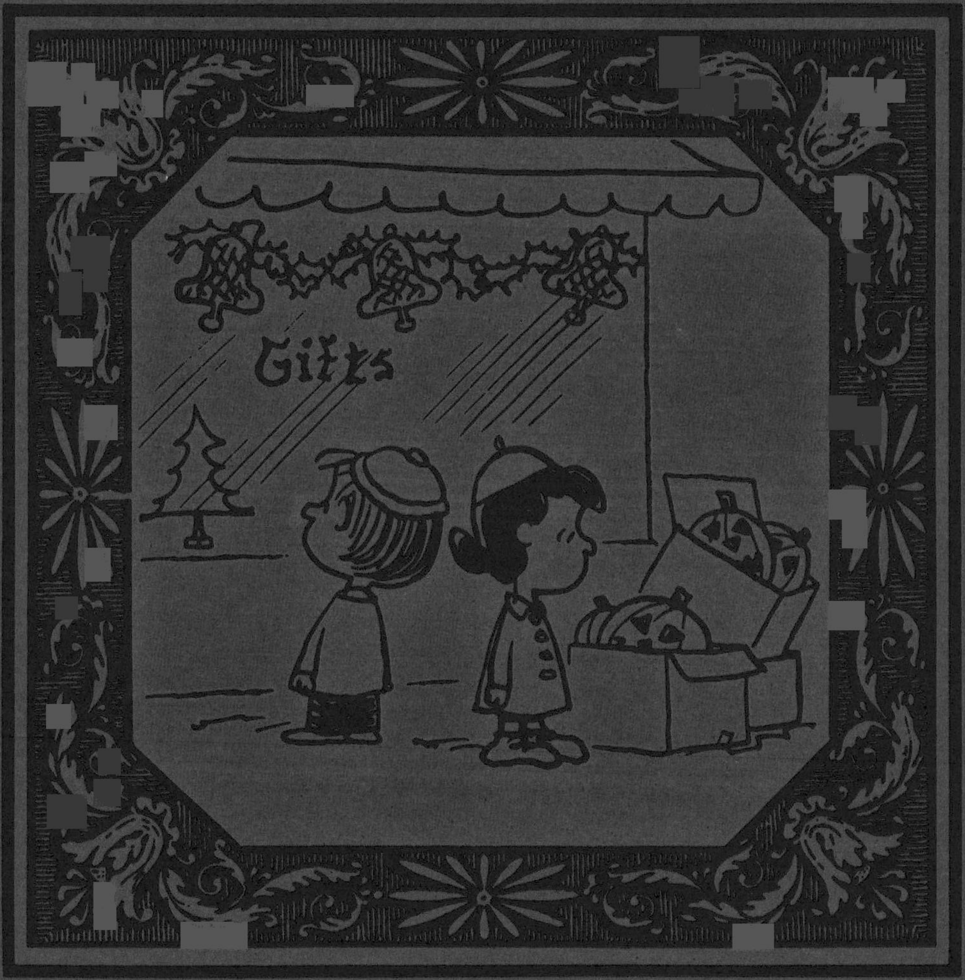
Gifts

Christmas is making a secret present for your dad at school, but it's always a calendar.

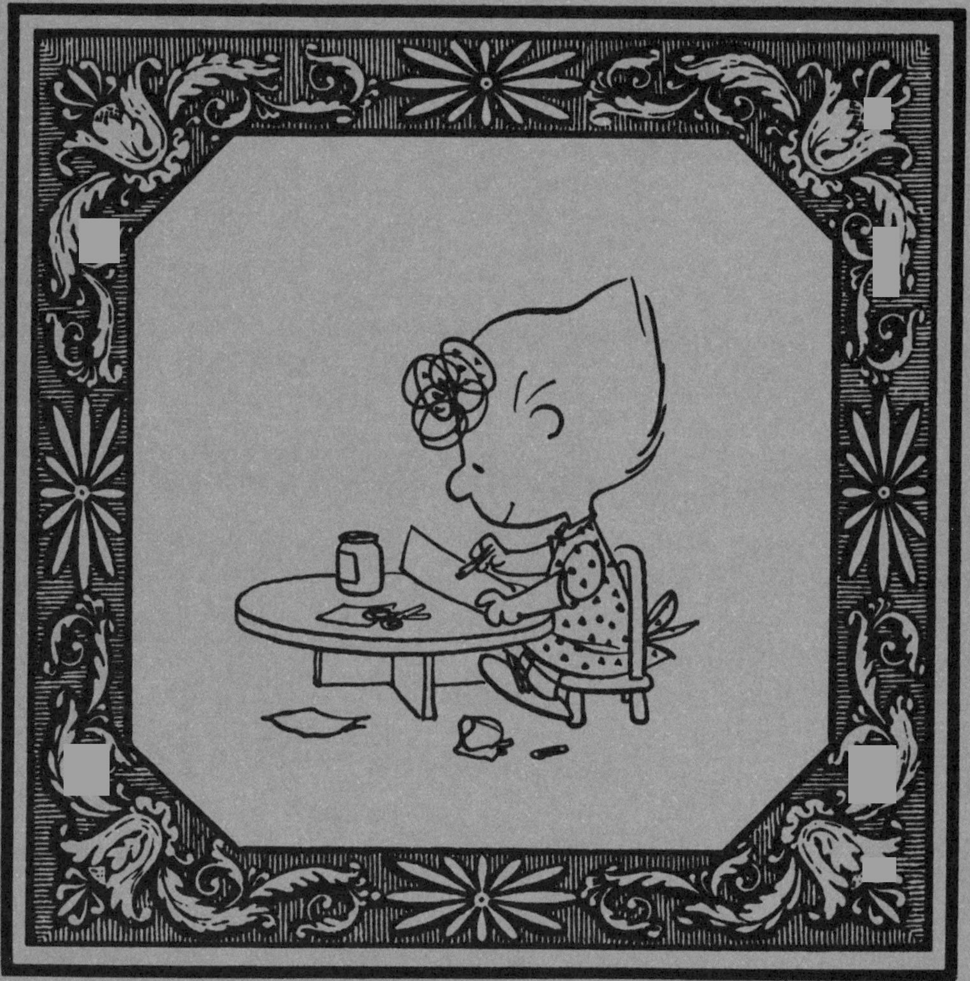

Christmas is that awful feeling that another year has gone by.

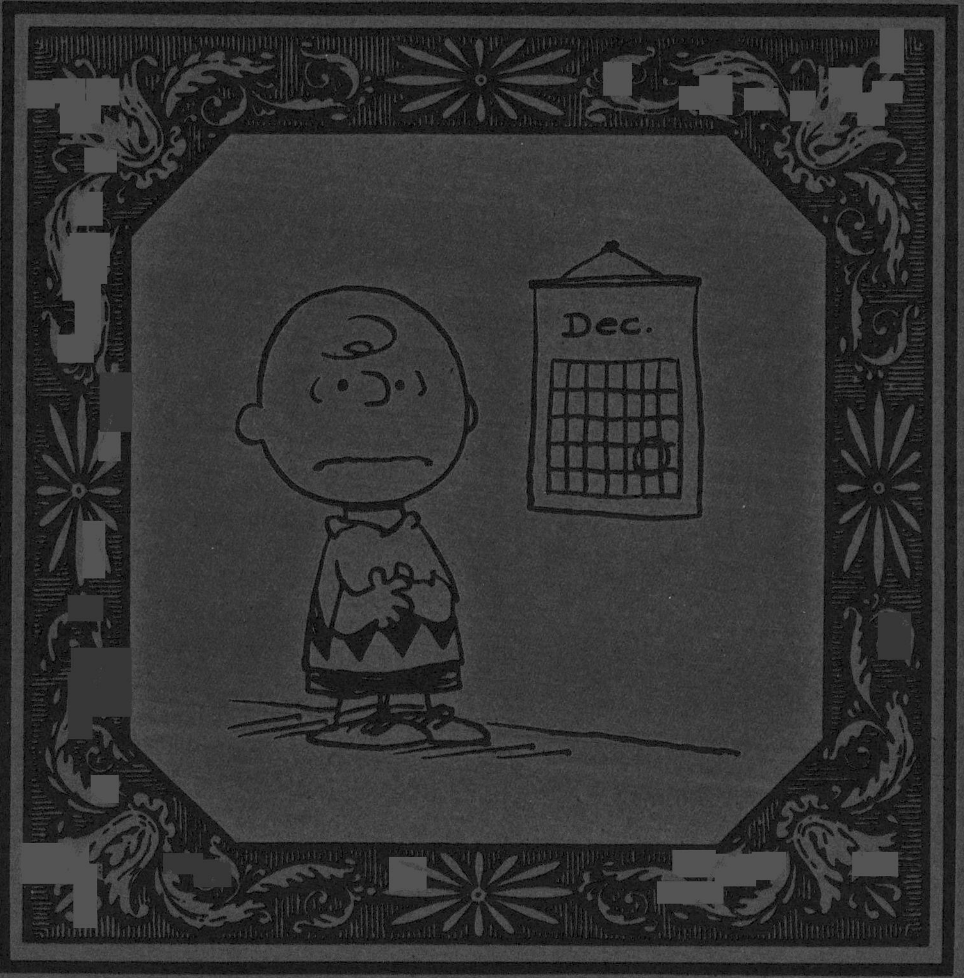
Dec.

Christmas is hearing about those partridges and pear trees until you're ready to lose your mind.

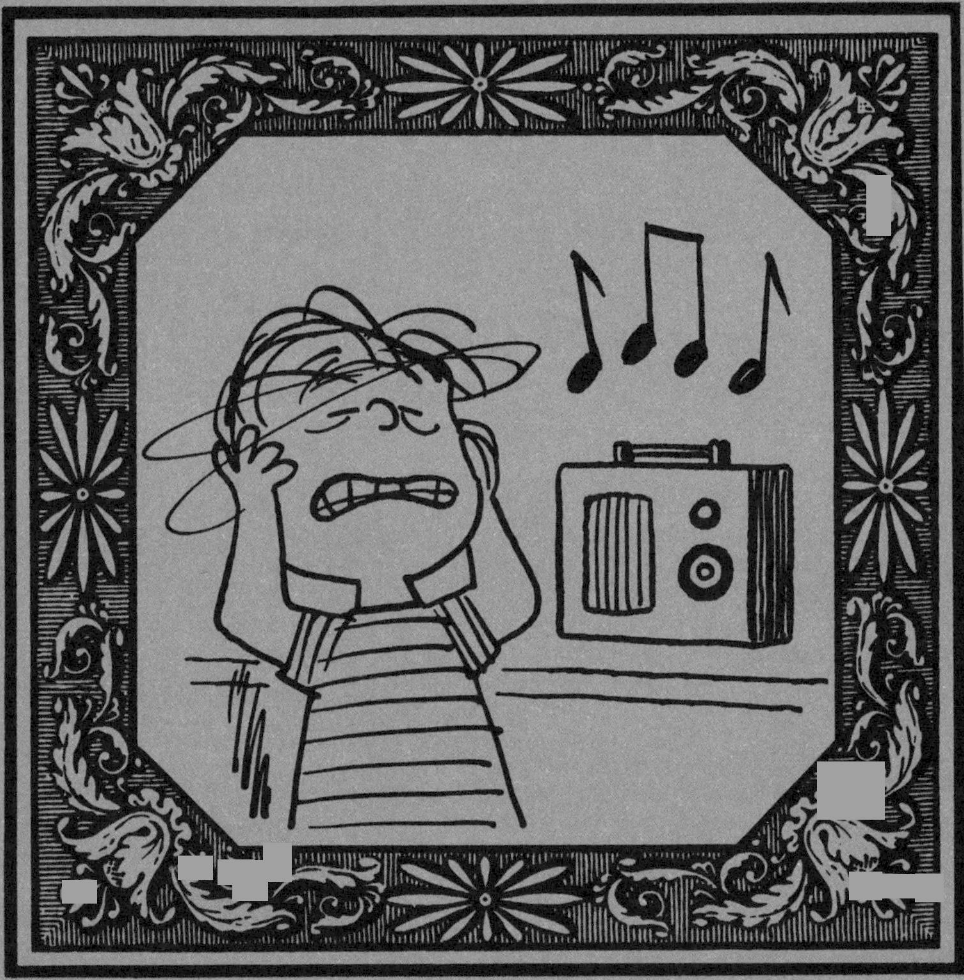

Christmas is a bowl of hard candy... that always sticks together.

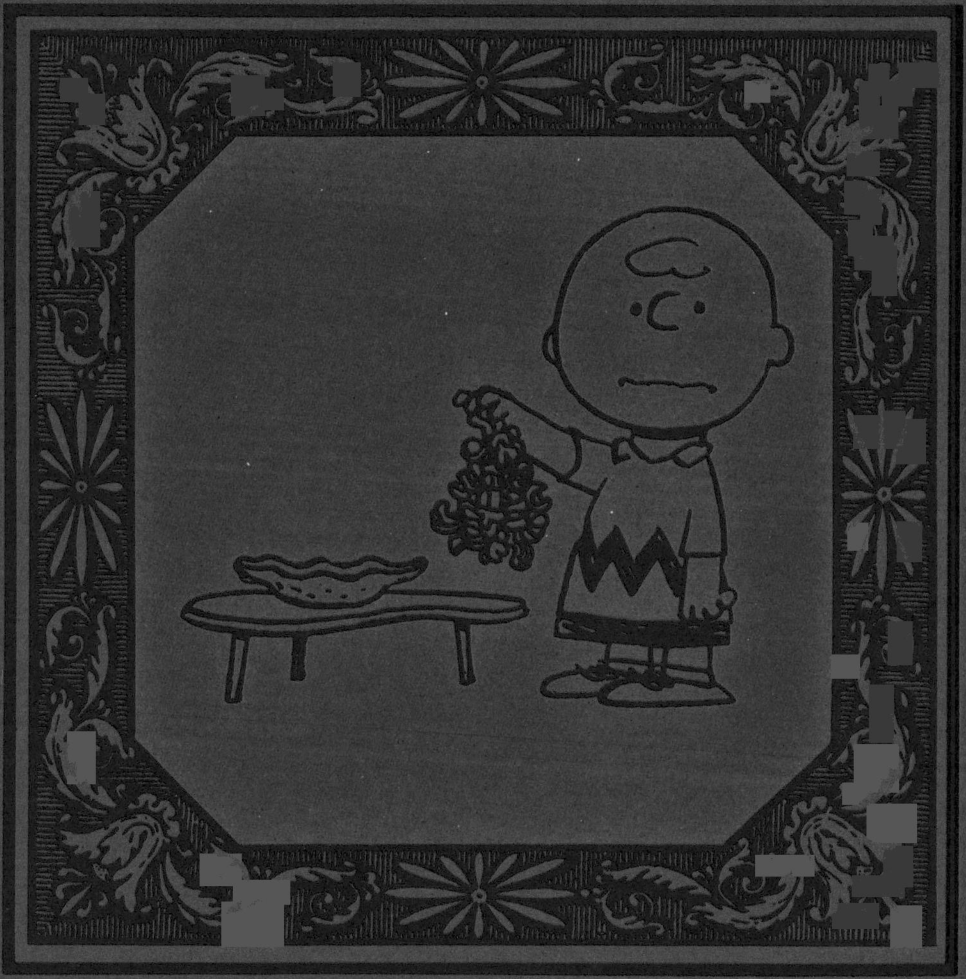

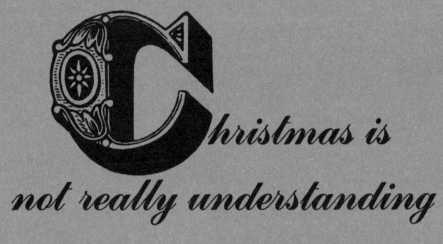

Christmas is not really understanding this business about the flying reindeer.

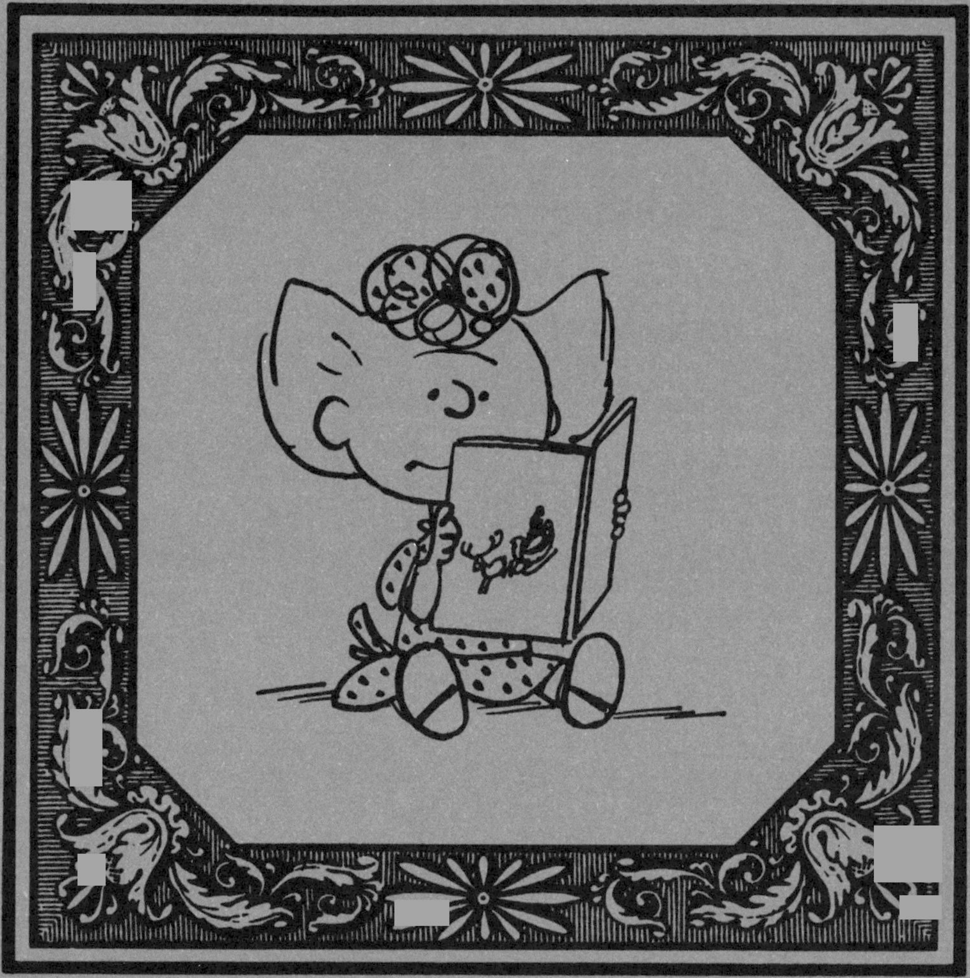

Christmas is when people say nice things to you who otherwise don't even know you're alive.

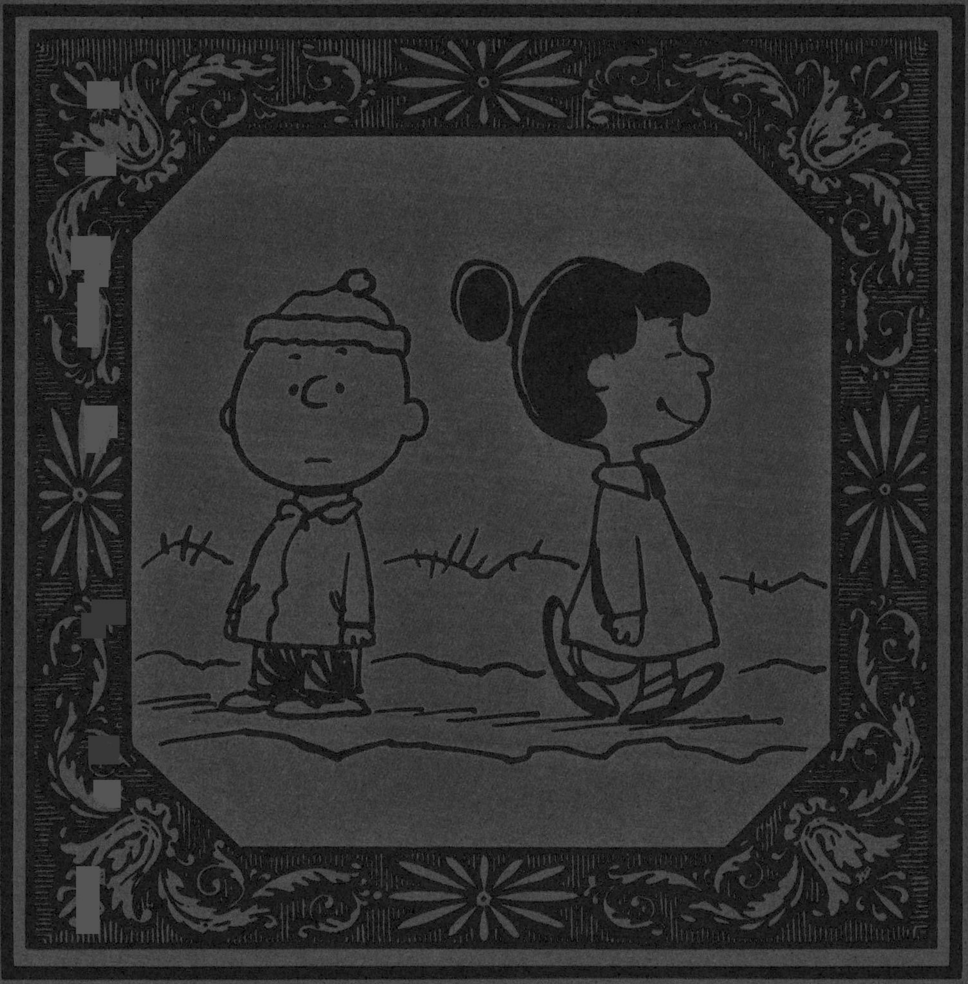

Christmas is

when you hug

your little

brother.

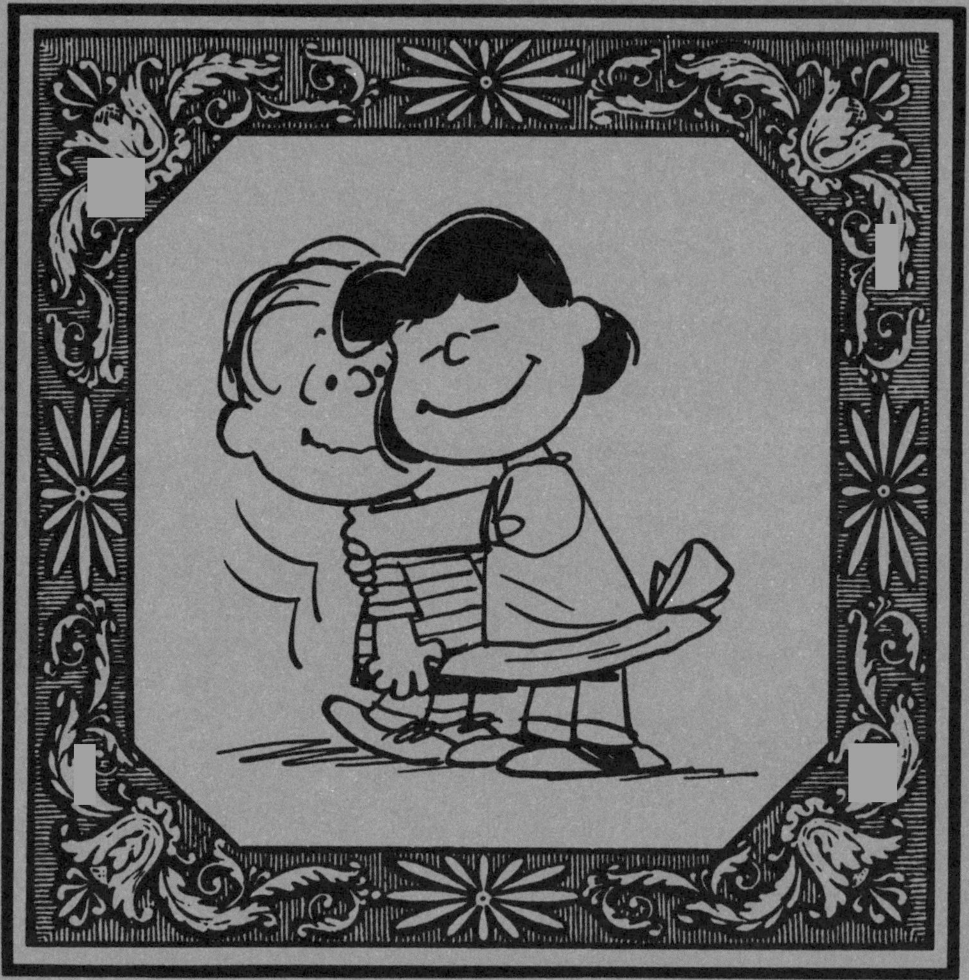

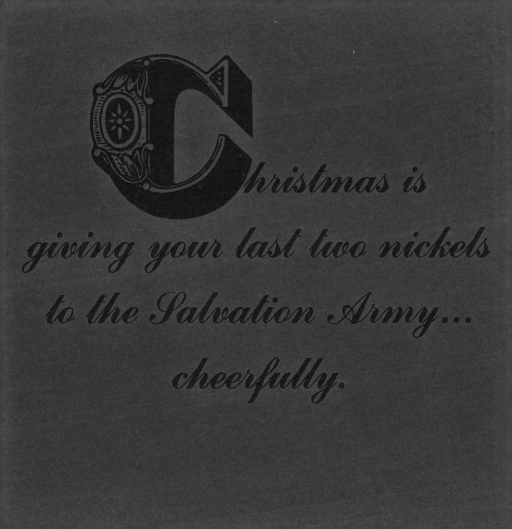

Christmas is giving your last two nickels to the Salvation Army... cheerfully.

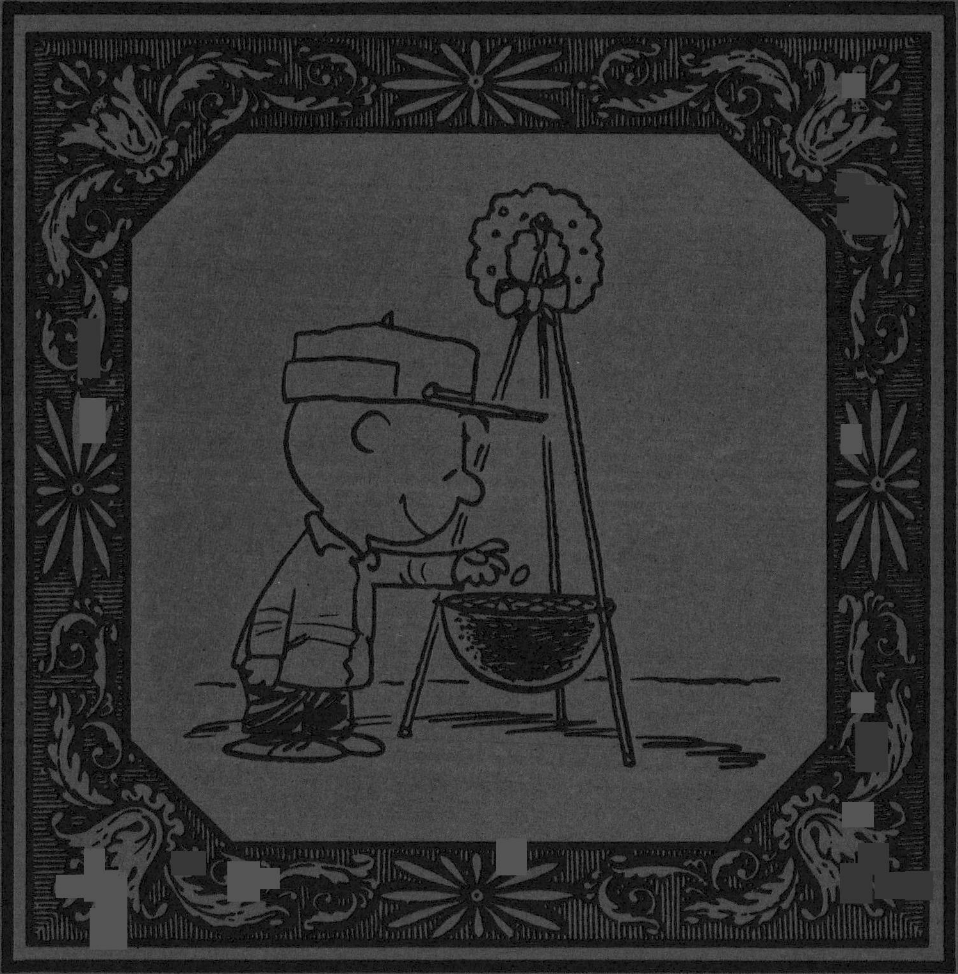

Christmas is
another box
of candied fruit
from your Aunt Agnes
in California.

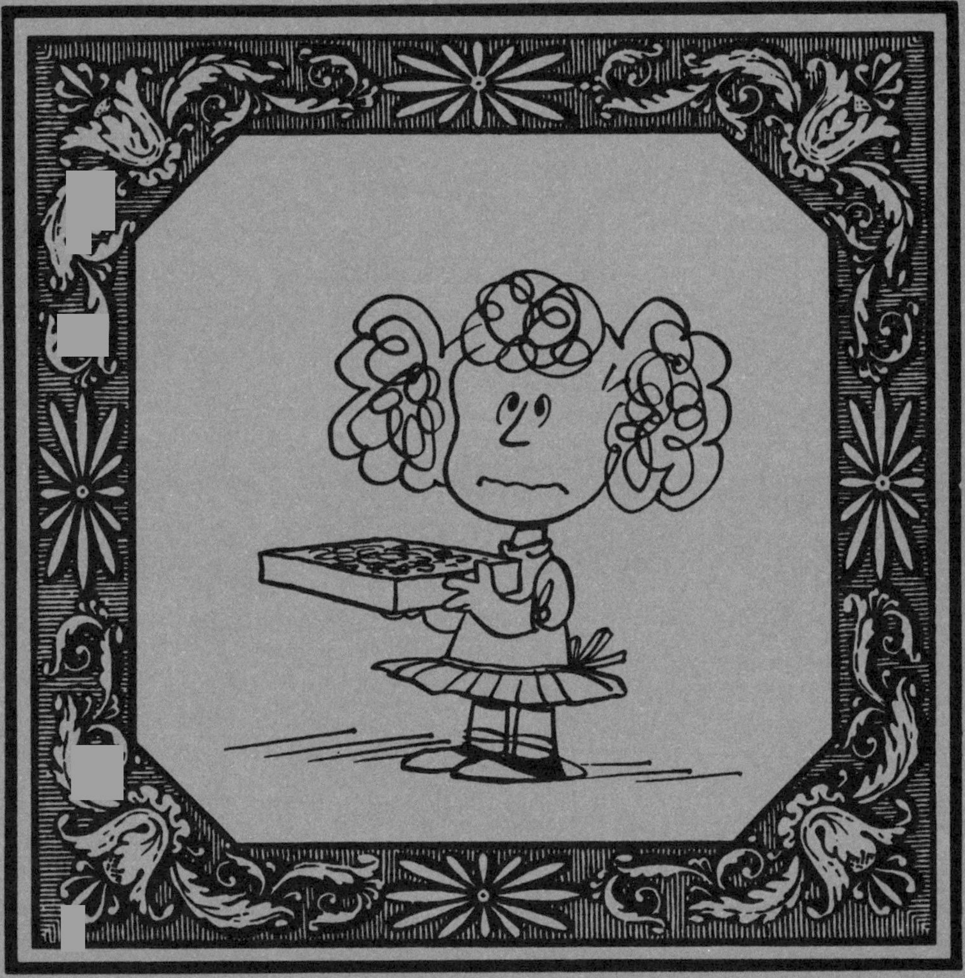

Christmas is getting all those cards from people you never sent any to!

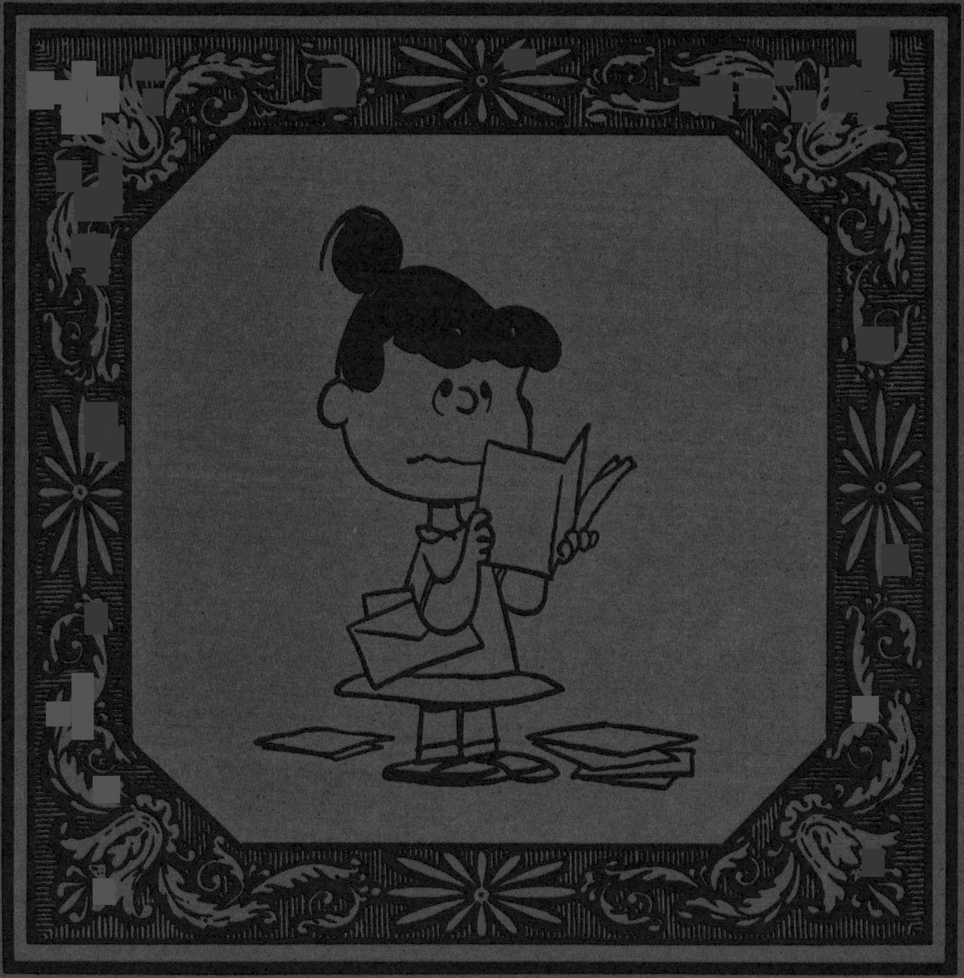

Christmas is
the church play...
But why do I always
have to be the shepherd?

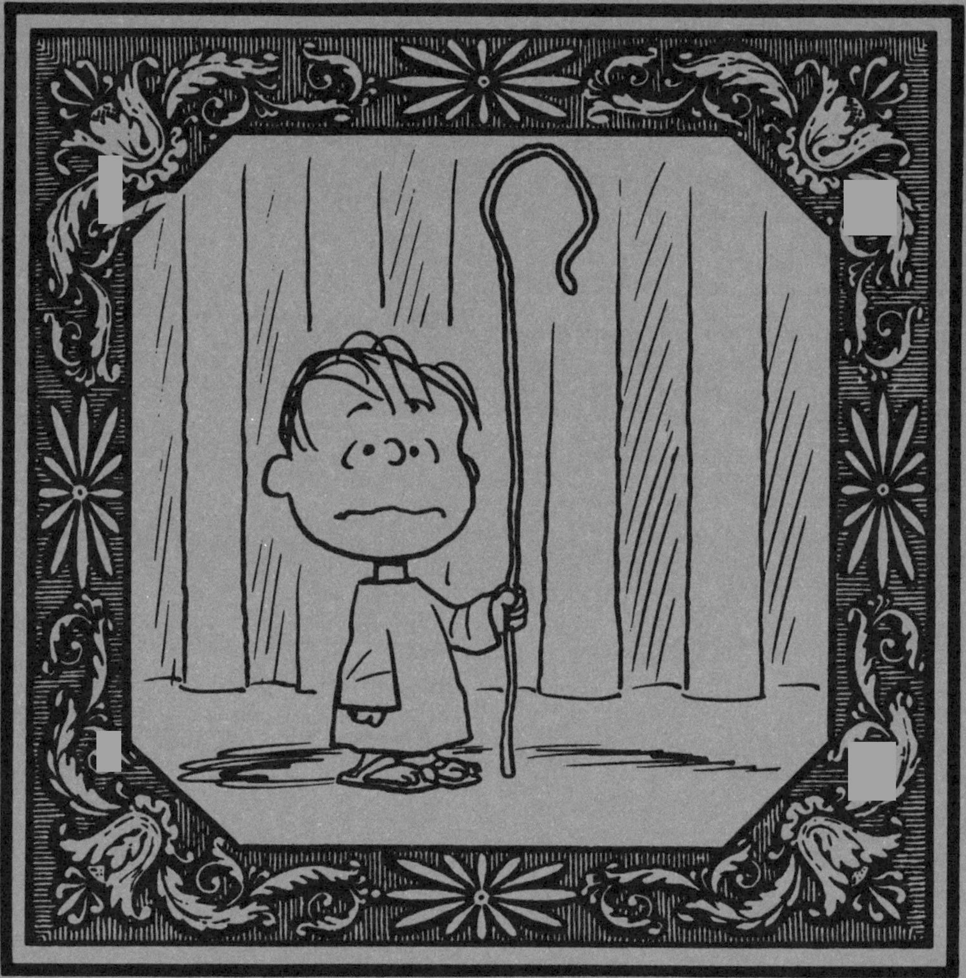

Christmas is losing your mother downtown in a crowded store.

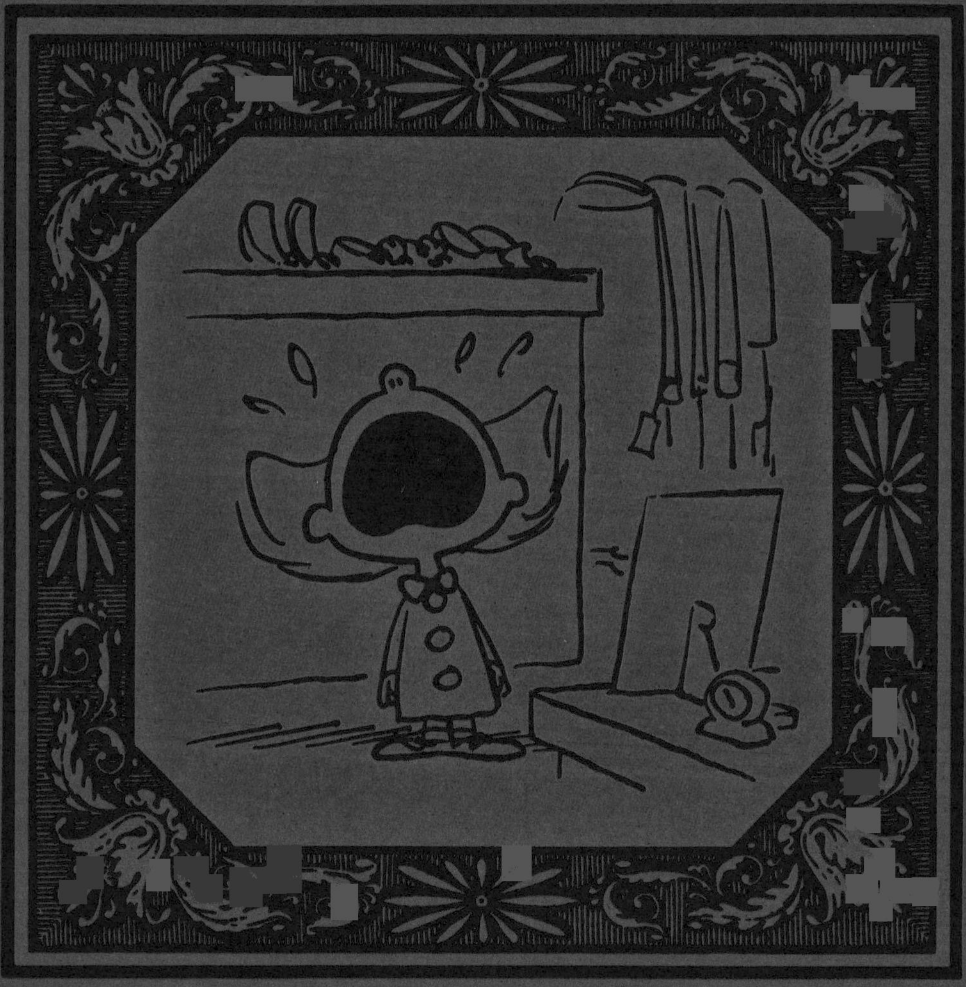

Christmas is buying your Mom something she's always wanted... a forty=nine cent bottle of bath salts.

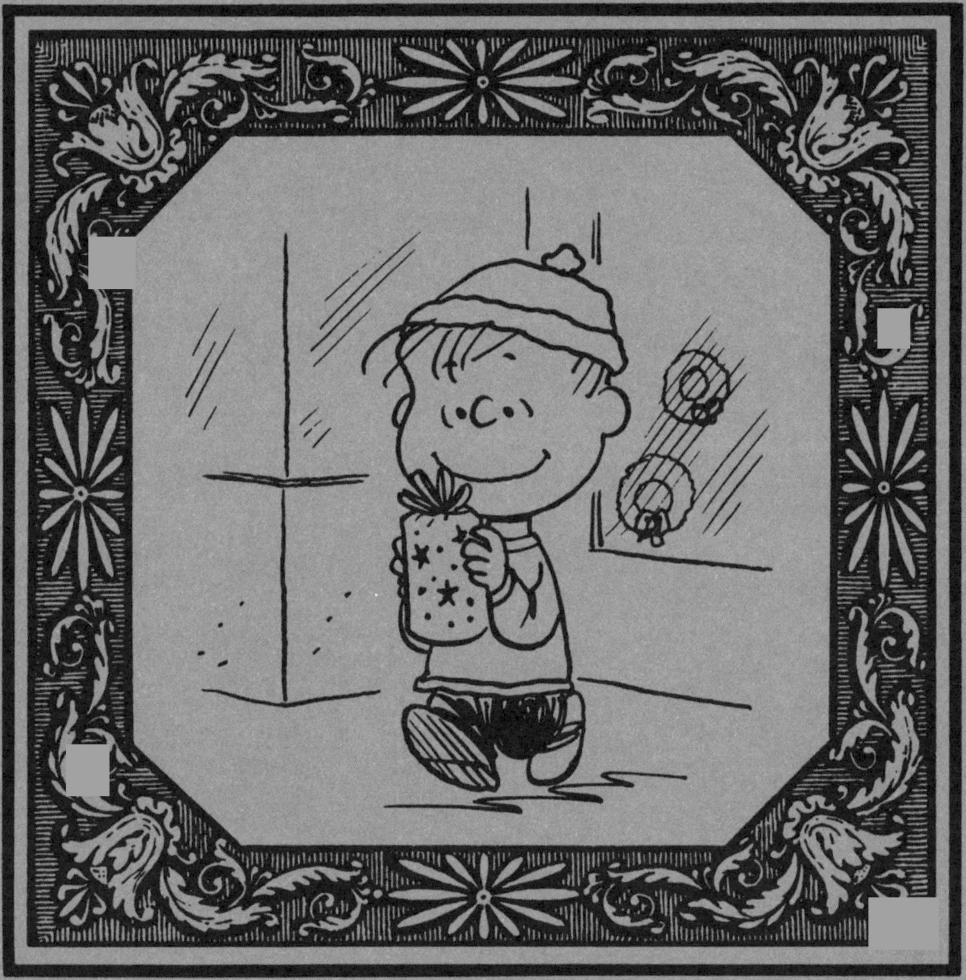

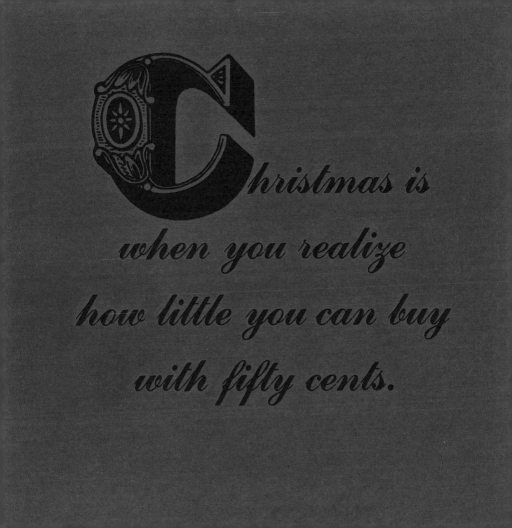

Christmas is
when you realize
how little you can buy
with fifty cents.

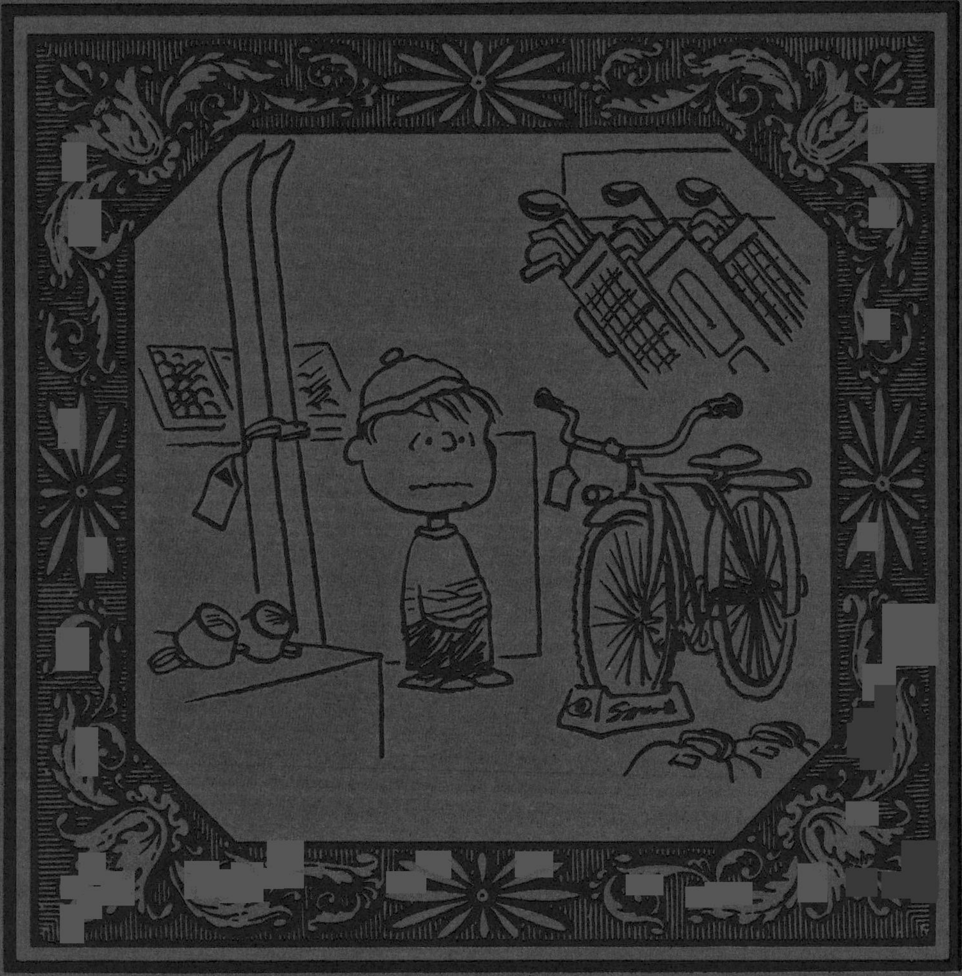

Christmas is wishing you had gotten this stupid present gift=wrapped.

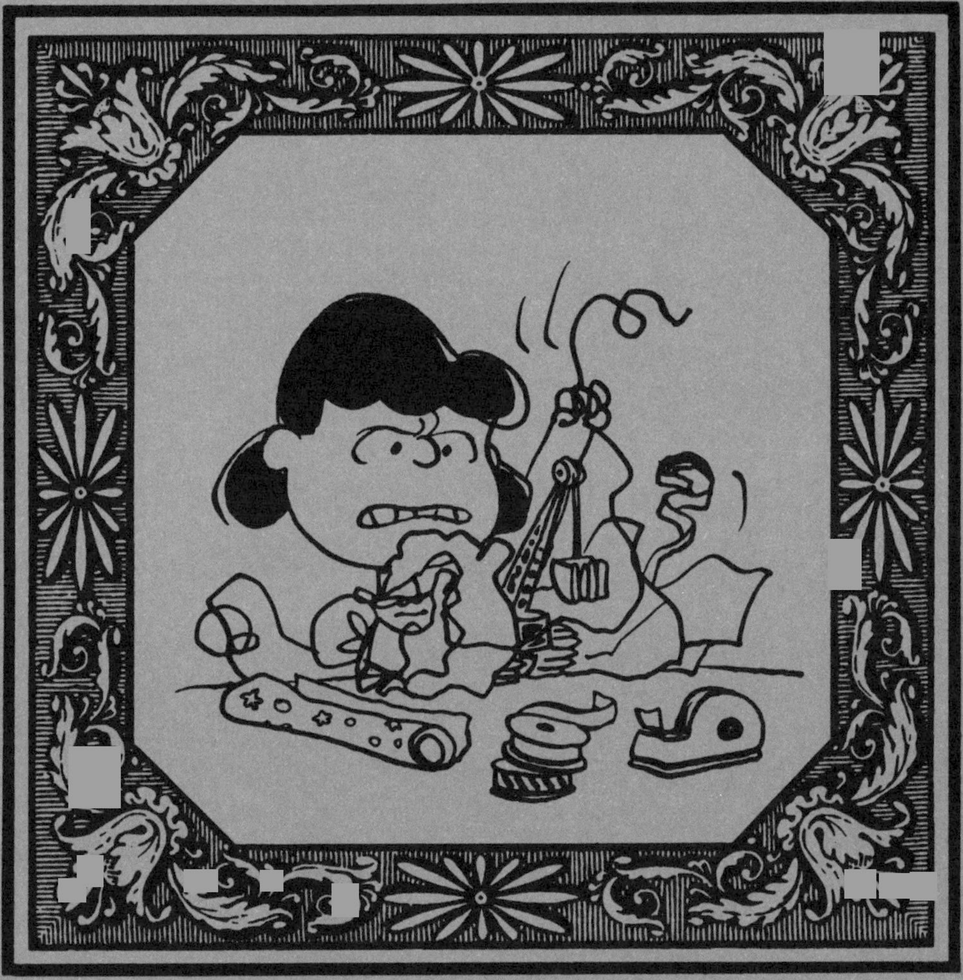

Christmas is
a box of tree ornaments
that have become
part of the family.

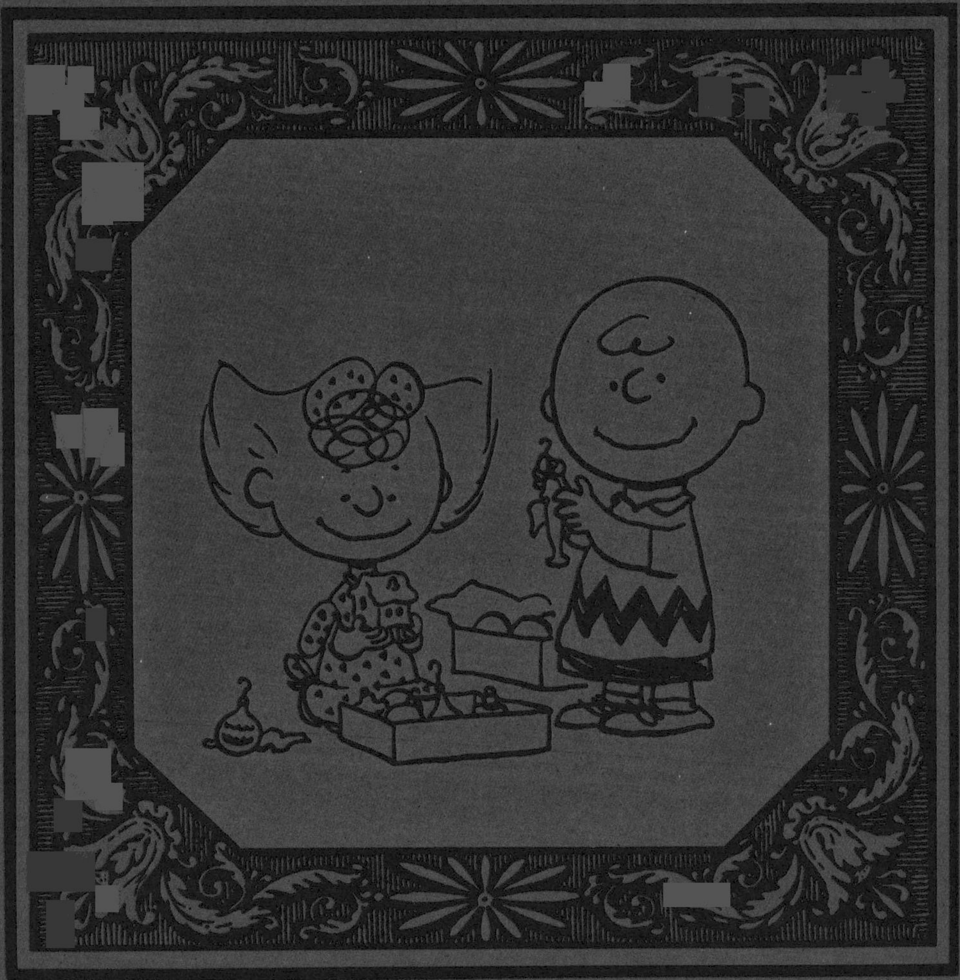

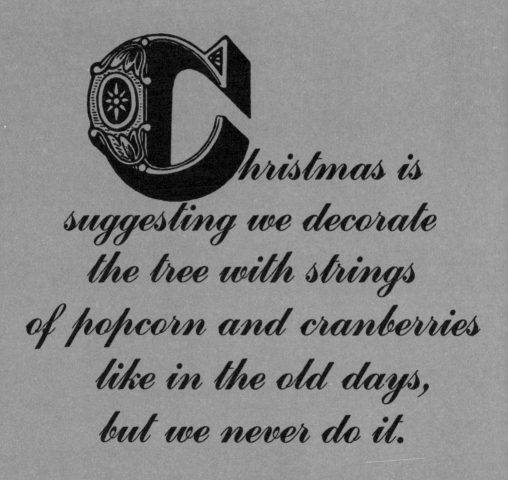

Christmas is
suggesting we decorate
the tree with strings
of popcorn and cranberries
like in the old days,
but we never do it.

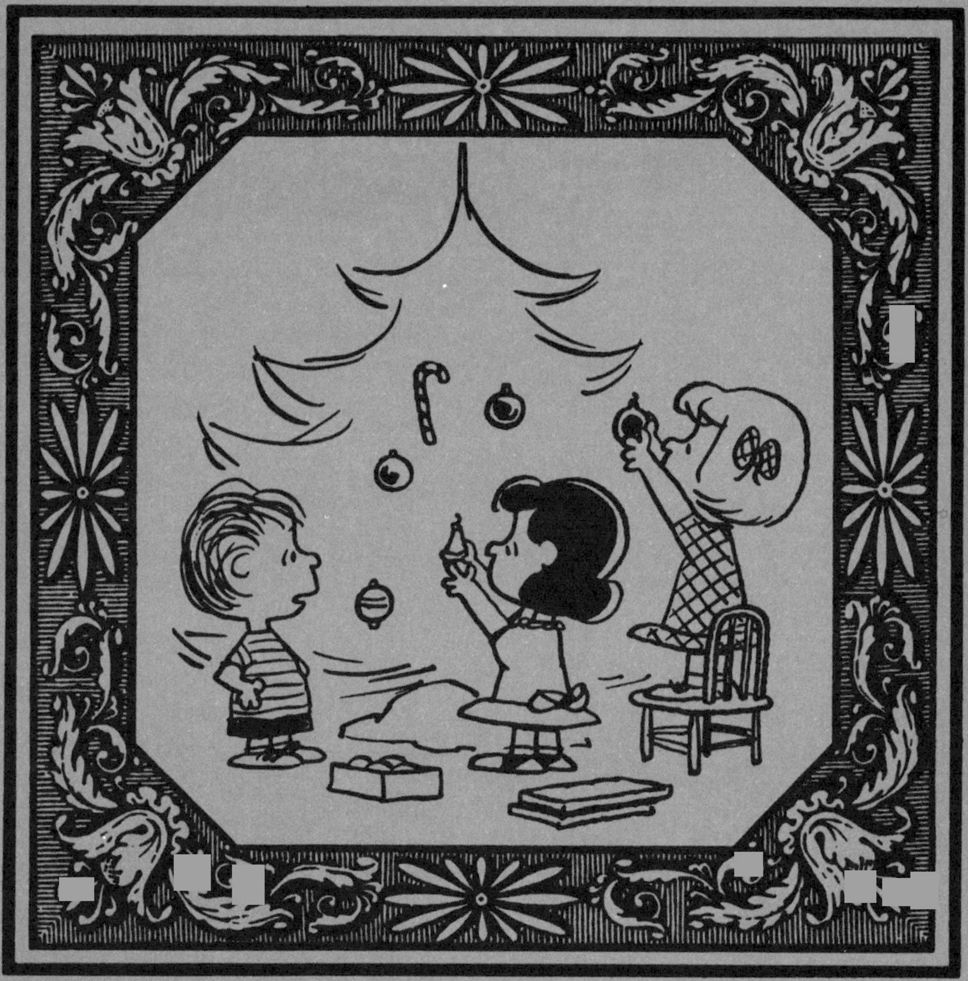

Christmas is wishing there really was such a thing as an old=fashioned Christmas.

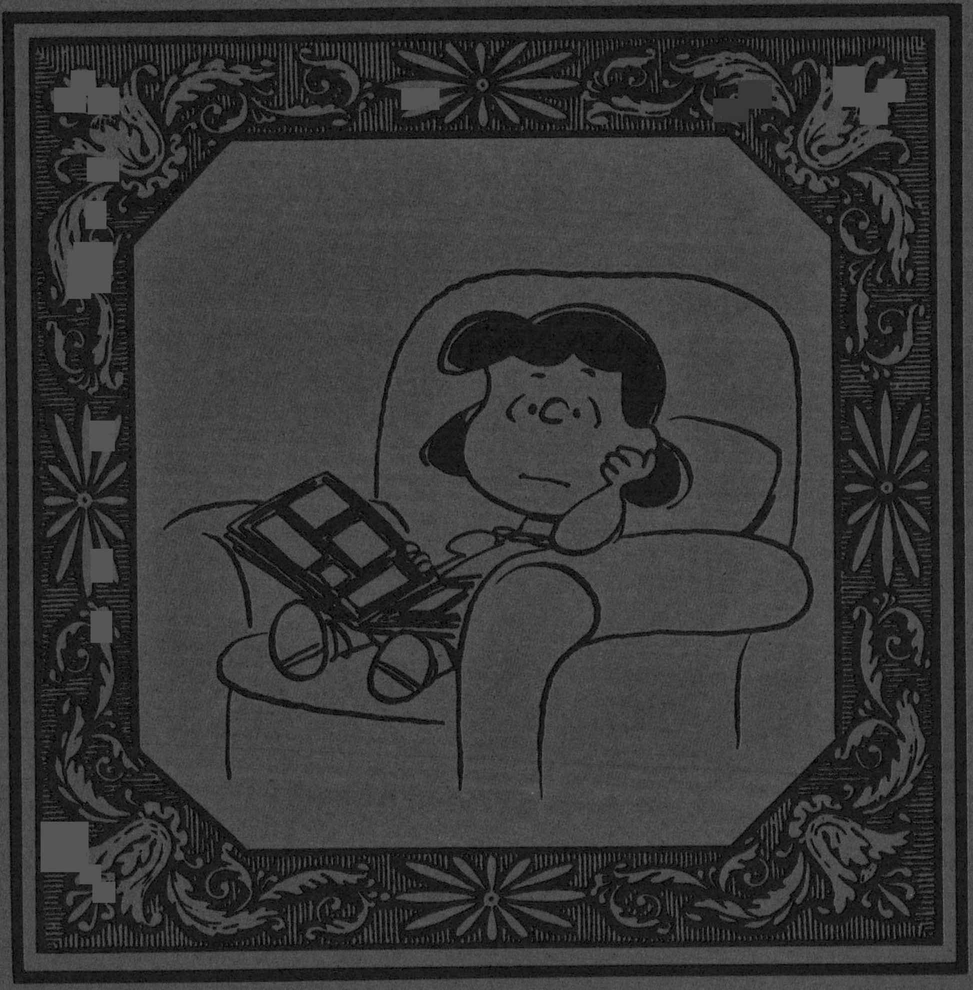

Christmas is

doing

a little something extra

for someone.

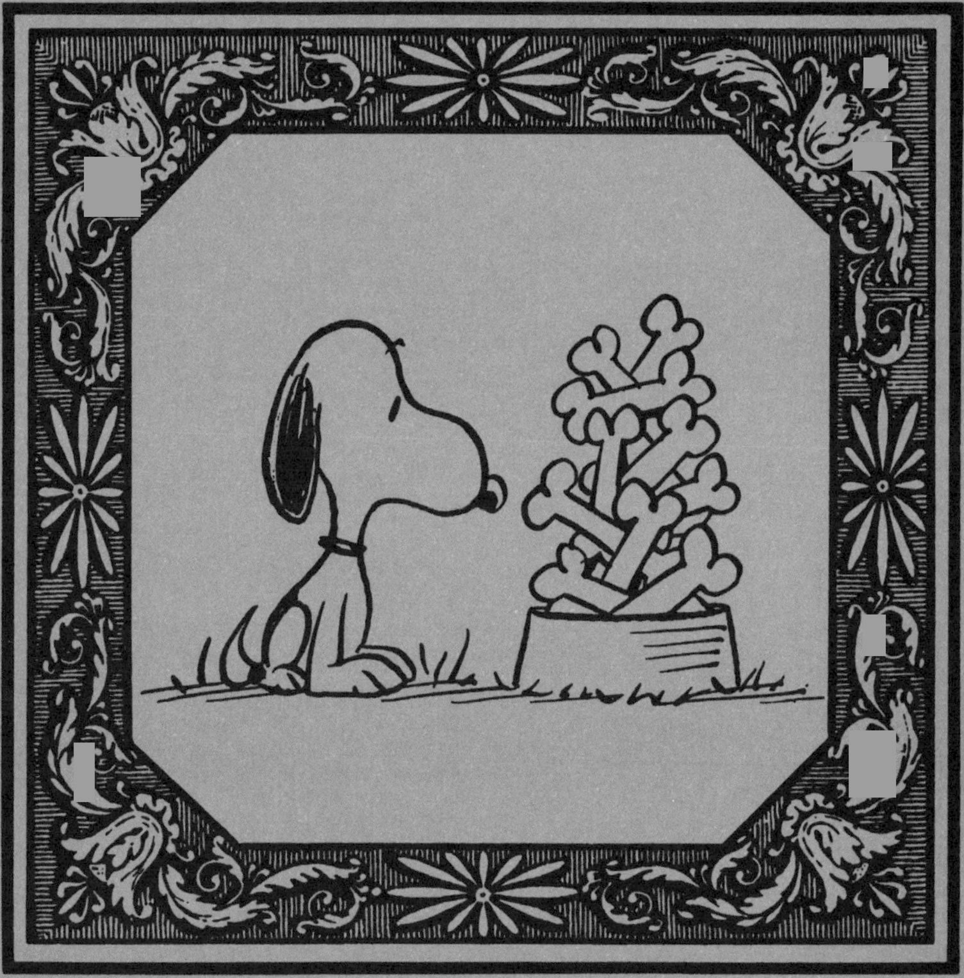

Christmas is a good day not to be in the hospital.

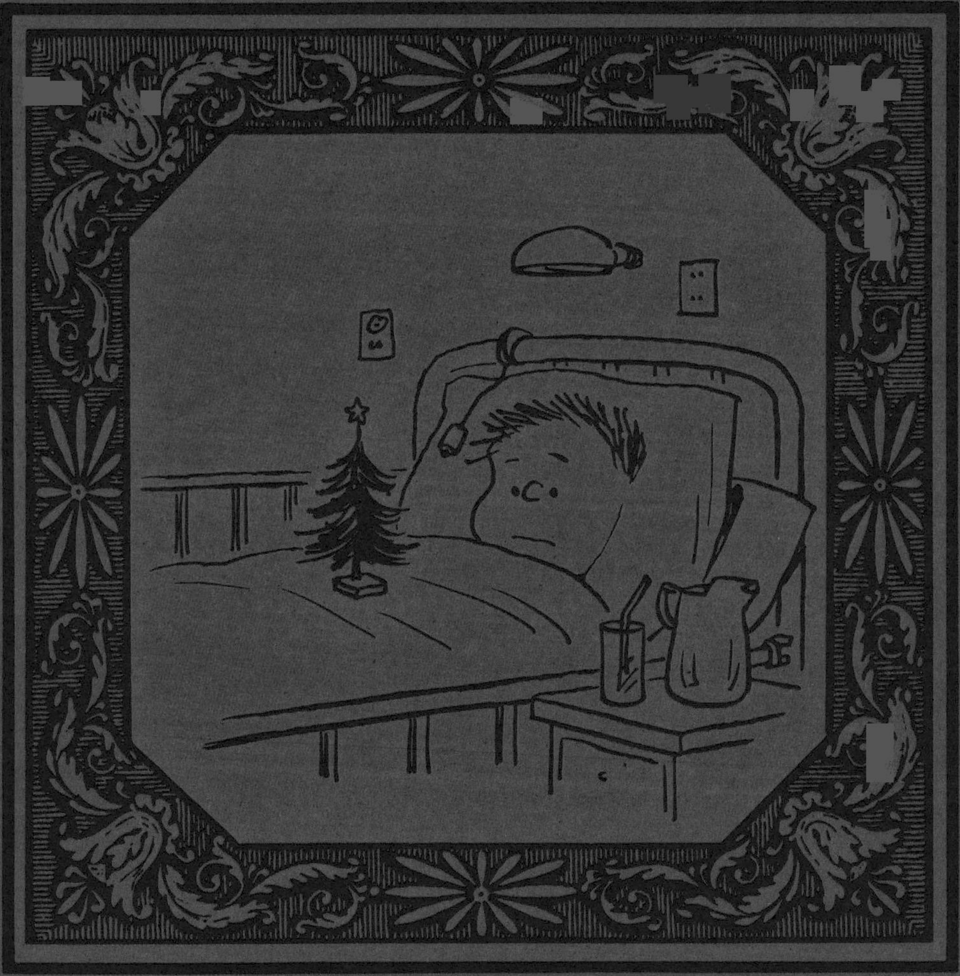

Christmas is going over the hills and through the woods to grandmother's house ...except she's moved to an apartment.

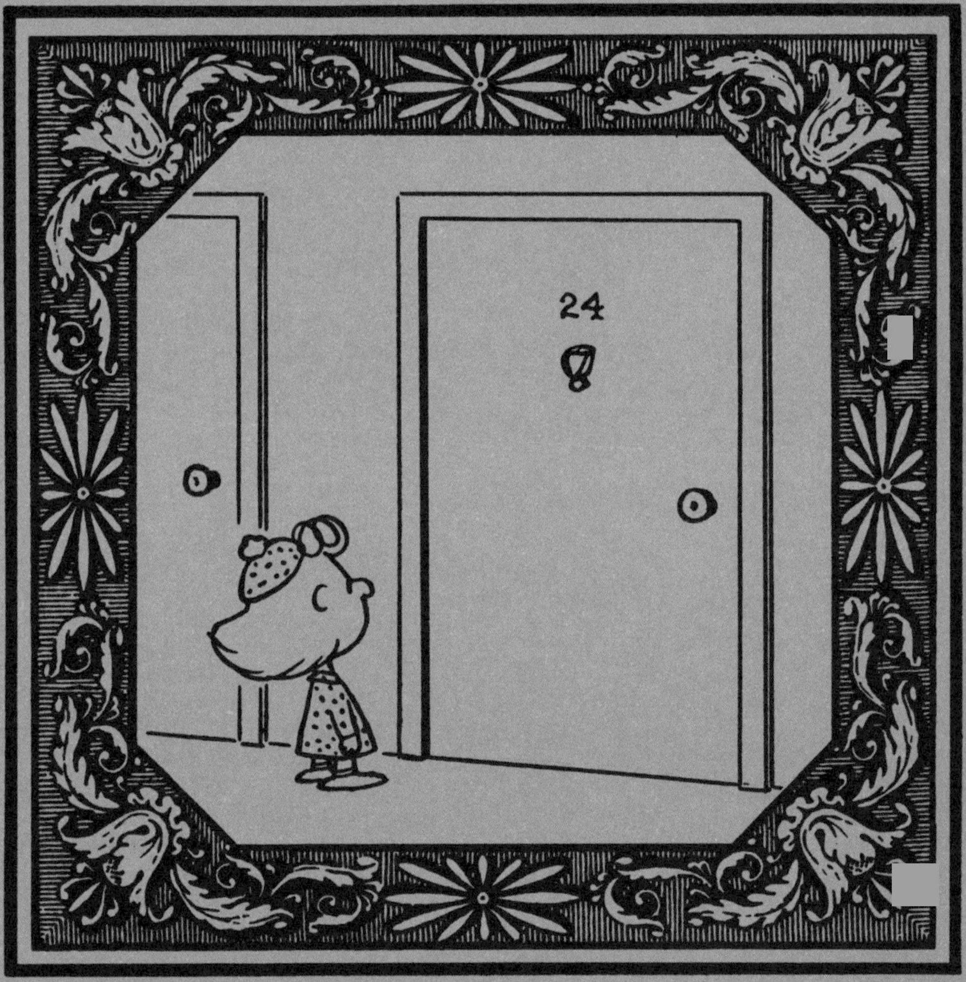
24

Christmas is

candy canes

and can't I eat

just one?

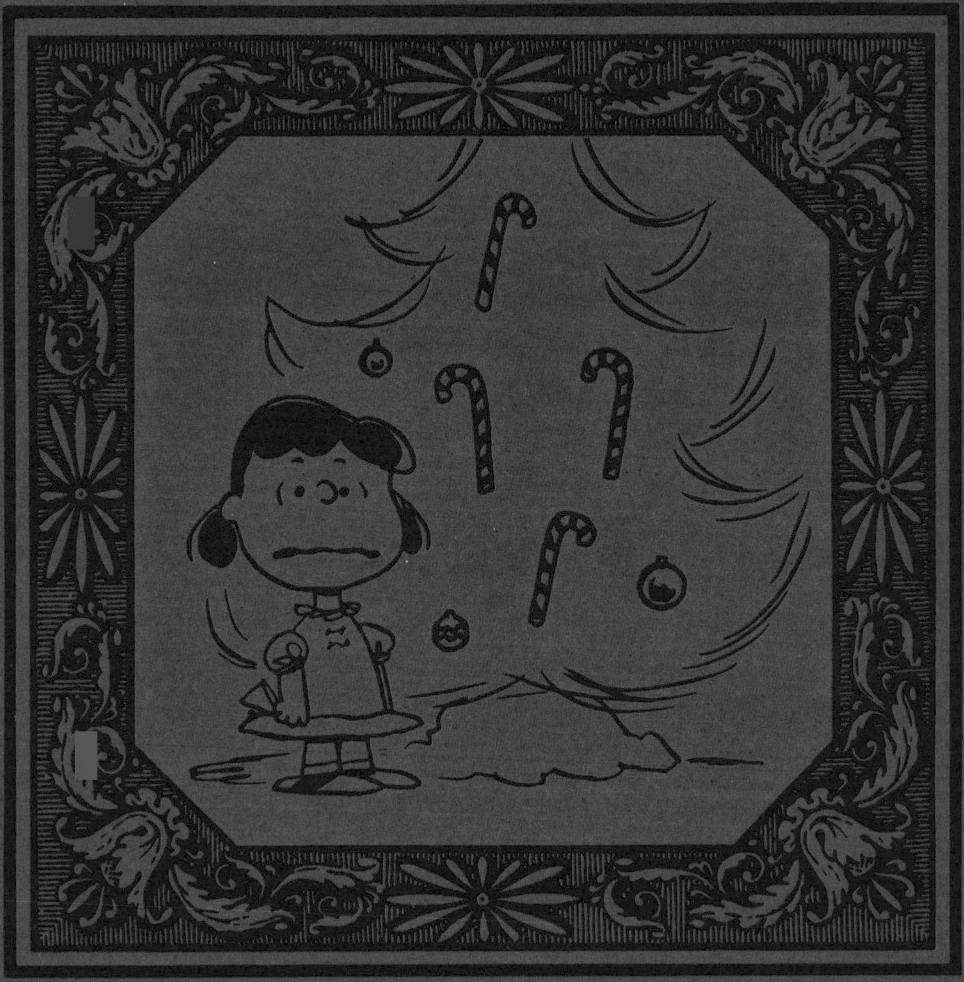

Christmas is
waiting for the grown-ups
to finish eating
so we can open
the presents.

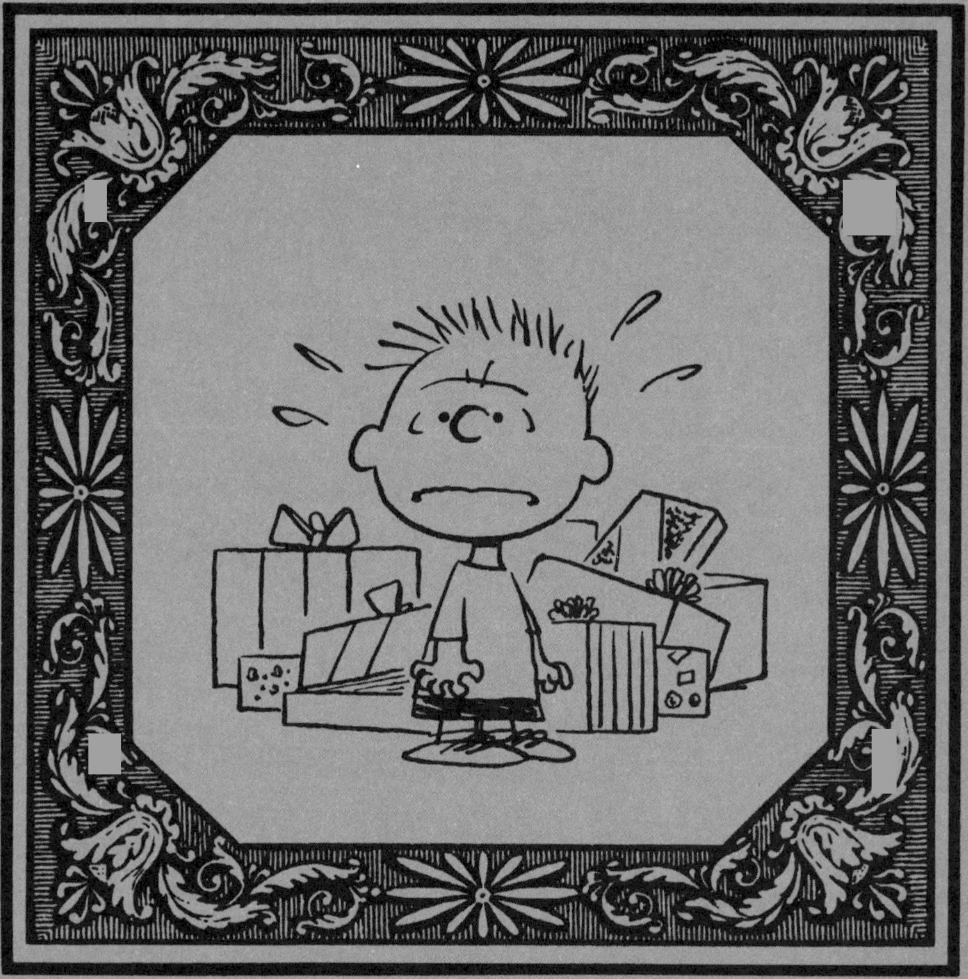

Christmas is the joy of giving, but getting is pretty good too.

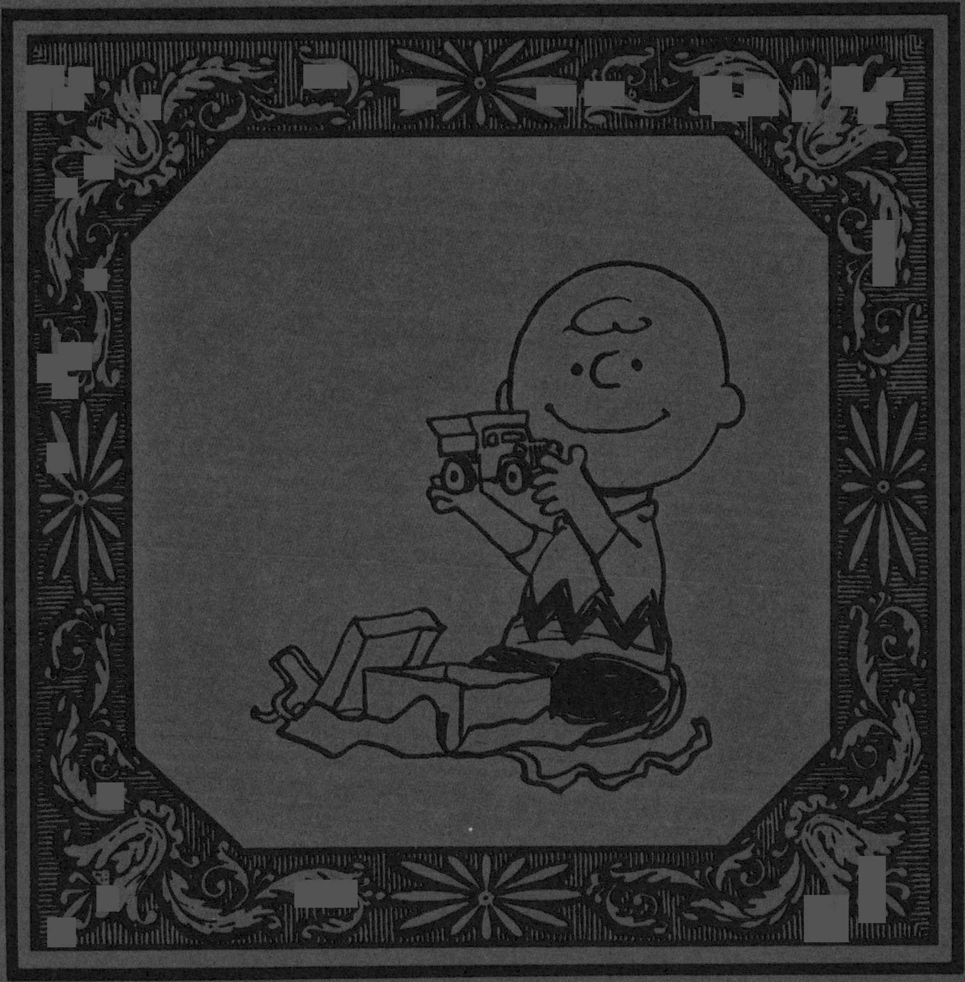

Christmas is watching the President light the tree on the White House lawn.

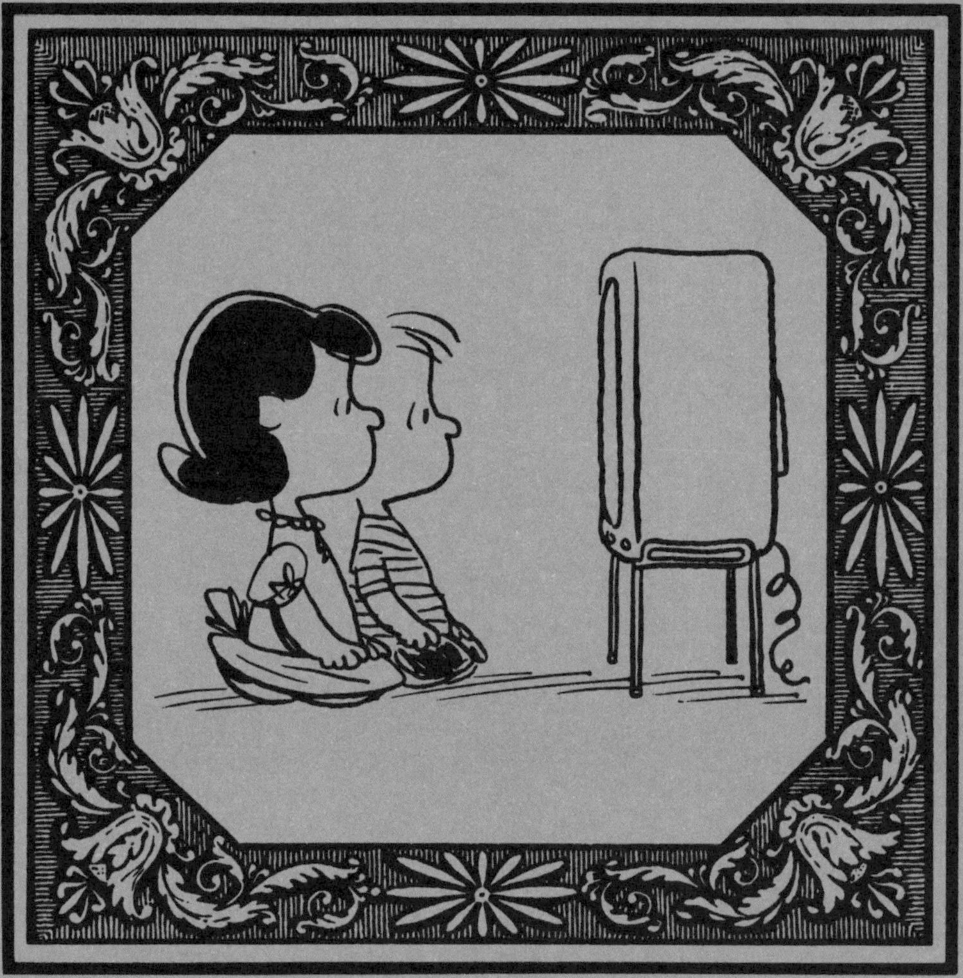

Christmas is
a time of waiting...
and waiting...
and waiting...
and waiting.

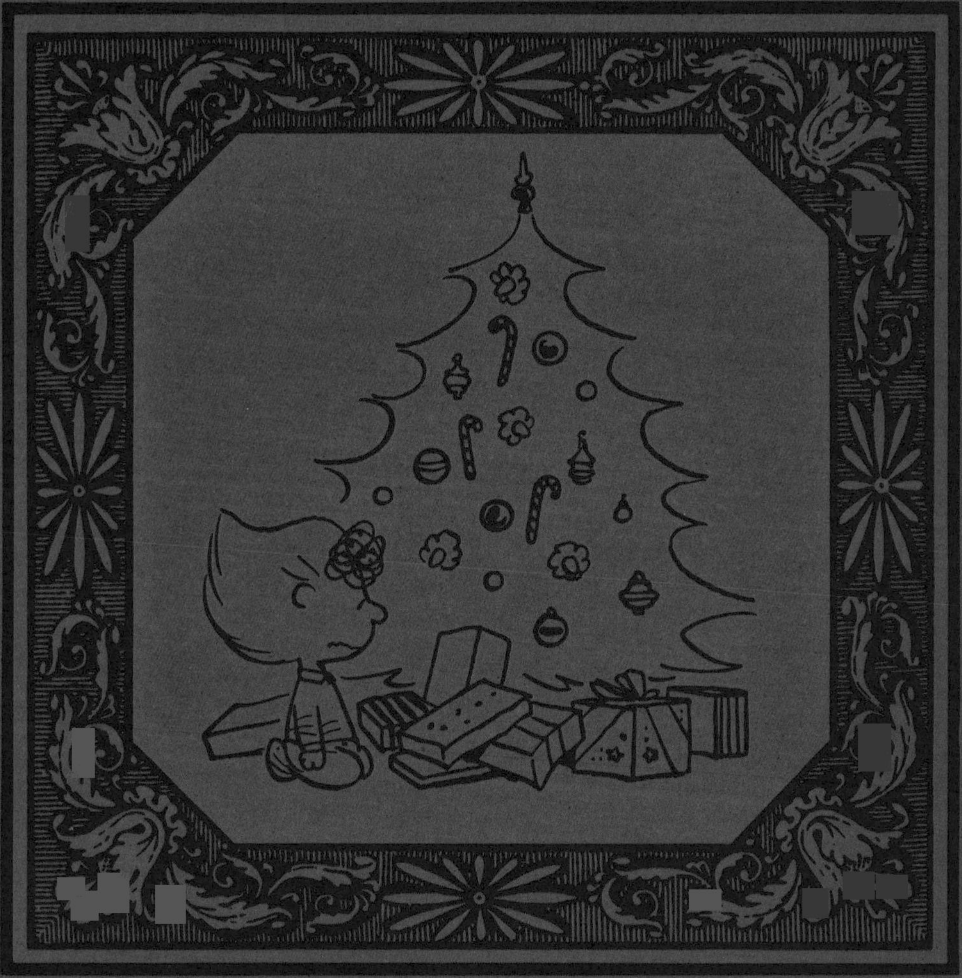

Christmas is wishing you could have seen the Star of Bethlehem.

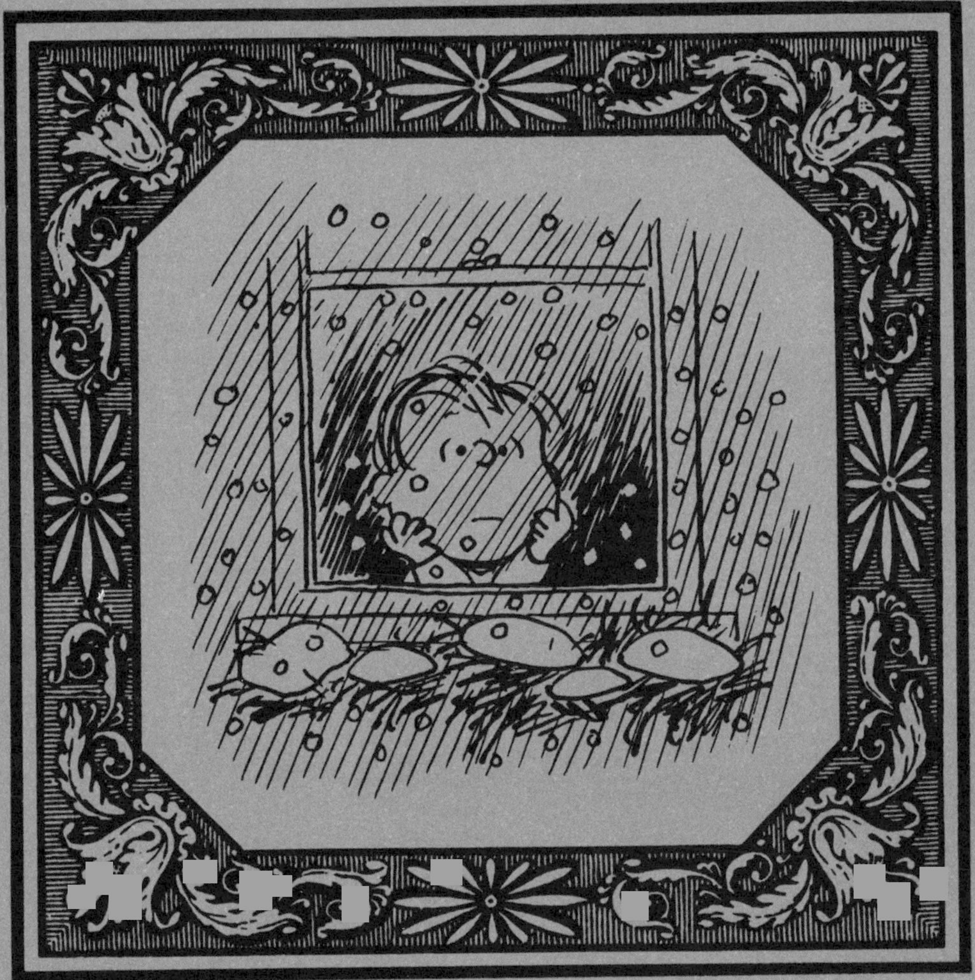

*Christmas is
a time of hope...
a time of loving...
a time of joy.*

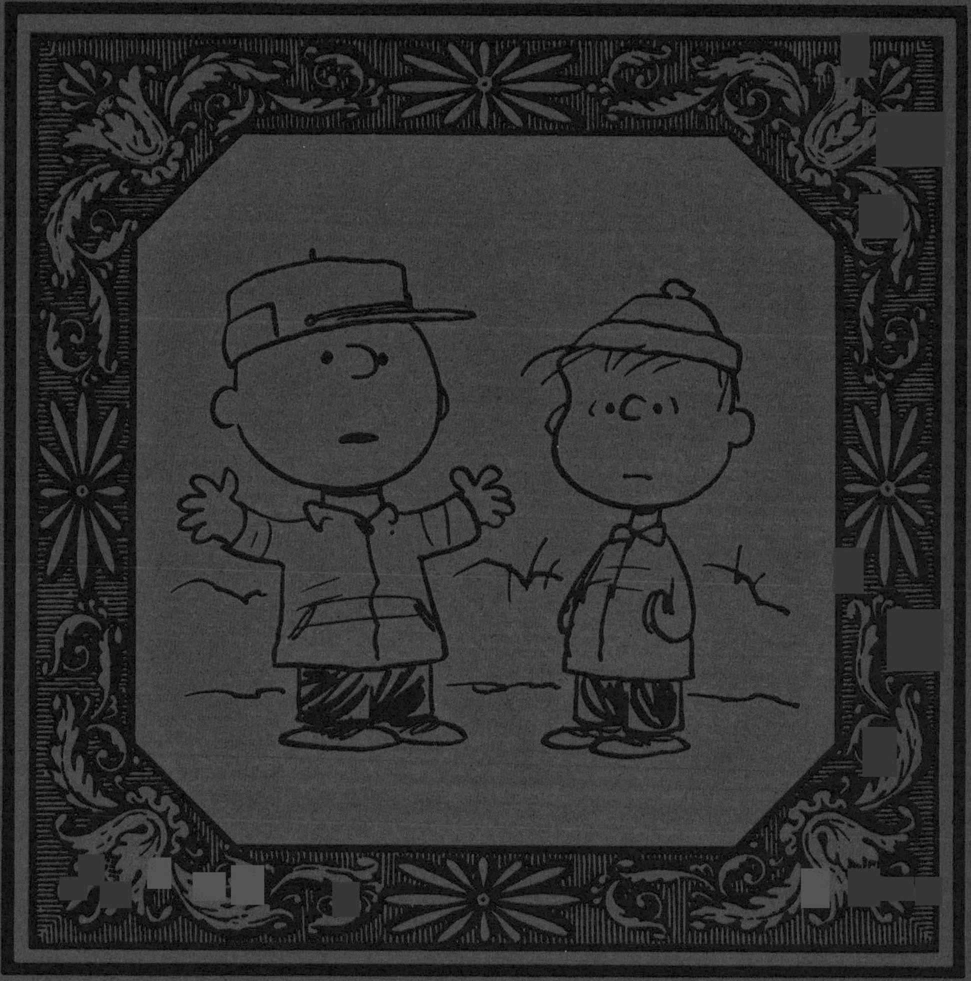

Christmas

makes the rest of the year

worthwhile.

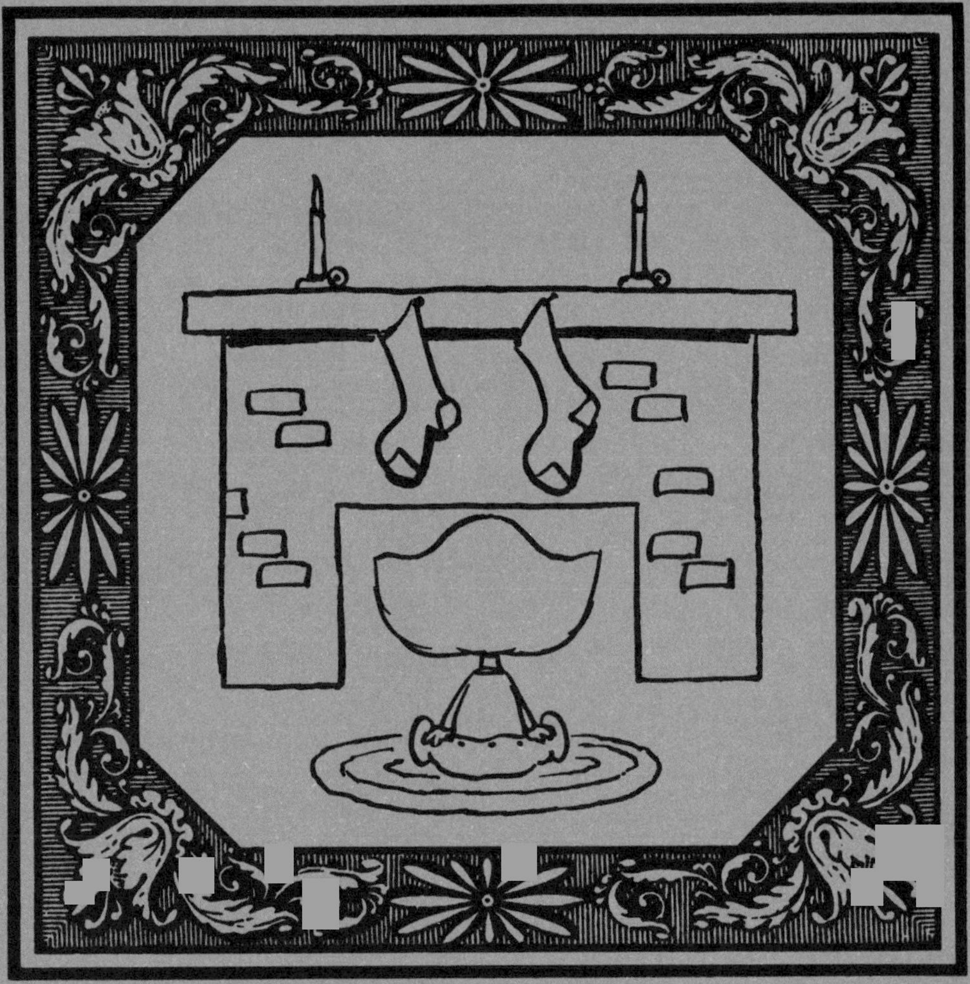

Other Books by Charles M. Schulz

Happiness Is A Warm Puppy

Home Is On Top of A Dog House

Security Is A Thumb and A Blanket

Happiness Is A Sad Song

Love Is Walking Hand In Hand

I Need All The Friends I Can Get

Suppertime

About Cider Mill Press Book Publishers

Good ideas ripen with time. From seed to harvest, Cider Mill Press strives to bring fine reading, information, and entertainment together between the covers of its creatively crafted books. Our Cider Mill bears fruit twice a year, publishing a new crop of titles each Spring and Fall.

Visit us on the web at
www.cidermillpress.com
or write to us at
12 Port Farm Road
Kennebunkport, Maine 04046

CIDER MILL PRESS
BOOK PUBLISHERS

Where Good Books are Ready for Press

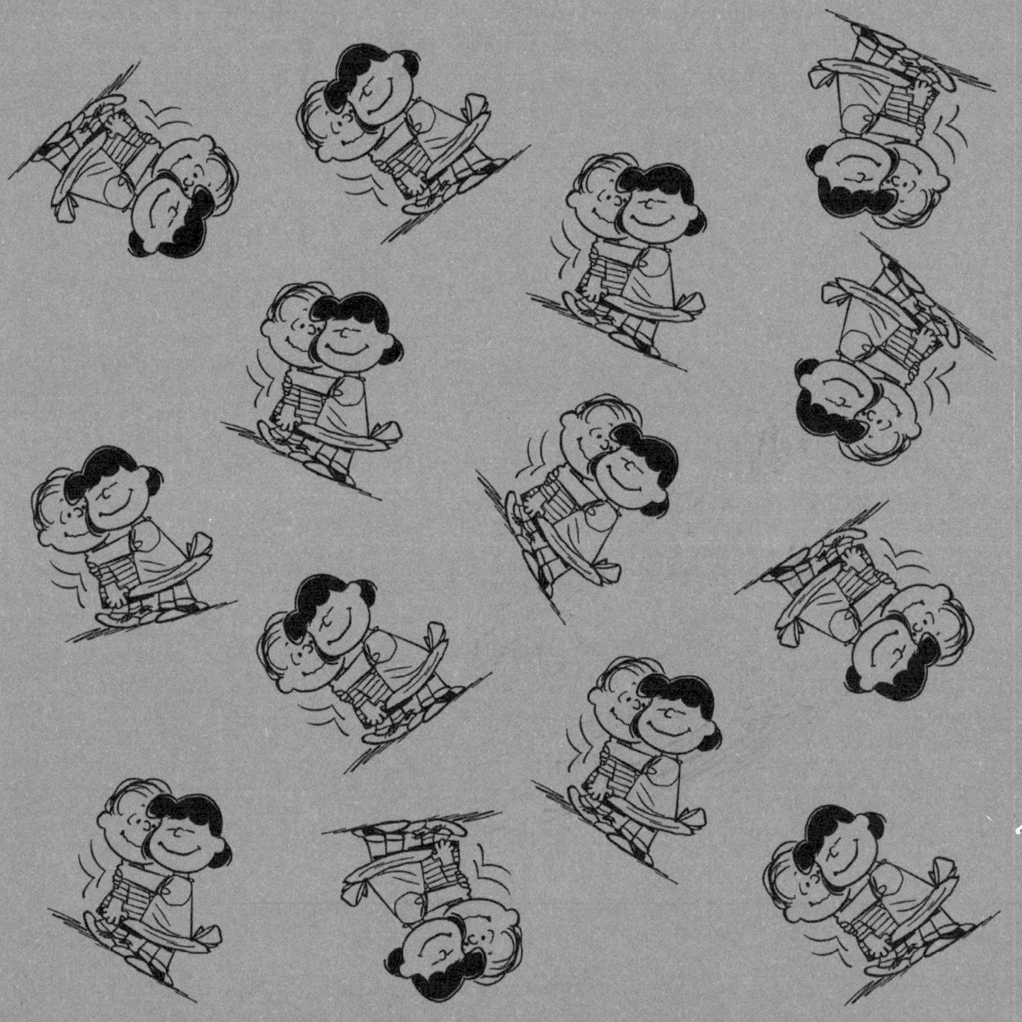